PICTURE THAT!
BATTLES
&WEAPONS

EXPLORING HISTORY THROUGH ART

CAROLINE CHAPMAN

MINNETONKA, MINNESOTA

Copyright © 2007 Two-Can Publishing and Toucan Books Ltd.

Two-Can Publishing
11571 K-Tel Drive
Minnetonka, MN 55343
www.two-canpublishing.com

Editorial Director: Jill Anderson

Created by
Toucan Books Ltd.
3rd Floor
89 Charterhouse Street
London EC1M 6HR

Project Manager: Ellen Dupont
Art Director: Bradbury and Williams
Editor: Donald Sommerville
Designer: Bob Burroughs
Proofreader: Marion Dent
Indexer: Michael Dent
Picture Researcher: Christine Vincent
Author: Caroline Chapman
Series Consultant: David Wilkins

ISBN 978-1-58728-588-2

Library of Congress Catalog Card Number: 2006033229

1 2 3 4 5 11 10 09 08 07 06

Printed in Singapore

Contents

Ancient Warfare

EVEN IN EARLIEST TIMES, WAR WAS BRUTAL. ARMIES OF THOUSANDS OF
MEN WOULD SLASH AND STAB EACH OTHER WITH SWORDS AND SPEARS,
WHILE DEADLY STONES AND ARROWS WHISTLED THROUGH THE AIR.

PICTURE THIS! IT IS THE YEAR 1469 B.C. You live in Karnak, a city on the Nile River in Ancient Egypt. Your father is a highly skilled carpenter. Right now he is building a two-wheeled, horse-drawn war chariot. To make it light and strong, he uses special wood.

Other craftsmen will work on the chariot too. A tanner will make leather cushions for the floor. A goldsmith will decorate it with gold, silver, and precious stones.

You would like to drive this war chariot into battle, but you are too young to be in the army, and chariots are too costly for anyone but kings.

This chariot has been ordered by the great pharaoh (or king) of Egypt, Thutmose III. He will ride north in it at the head of his army to fight an enemy tribe. This conflict, called the Battle of Megiddo, will be the first battle recorded in history.

Before your time, people fought with sticks and stones, or even with their bare hands. As they moved into towns, they formed armies to defend themselves and to mount attacks on enemies. The first armies were created in Ancient Mesopotamia (present-day Iraq) and in your homeland of Egypt.

War chariots are the most advanced military machines of your time. Thutmose's army has

THIS WOODEN TOMB model shows Egyptian soldiers armed with spears and shields. To figure out how many enemy soldiers they have killed in a battle, the Egyptians cut off one hand from each dead enemy and then count the hands!

THIS BRONZE HELMET was made in Greece about 2,500 years ago. Only the eyes and mouth are left unprotected. A row of men in these helmets marching towards you in battle would have been terrifying.

thousands of chariots. But the army's most powerful weapon in battle is the bow, which can be fired from a chariot—like the one your father is building—or from horseback.

Another fearsome weapon of your time is small enough and simple enough that you may already know how to use it. A sling—made out of linen, leather, or other flexible materials—has a pouch to hold a stone and long cords to allow for throwing. A skilled slinger can hurl a sharp stone 400 feet (130 m) toward the enemy.

Your sling and the war chariot your father is building are powerful weapons. But as time goes on, wars, weapons, and battles become more complex. In Ancient Greece, rather than relying on long-range weapons like the bow and sling, soldiers will fight at close range. They wield spears and swords and wear heavy armor. Ancient Greek armies will be the first to teach their soldiers to fight in regular formations some time before the year 600 B.C.

The great armies formed after that will conquer huge empires covering large parts of Europe, the Middle East, and Africa. In the 300s B.C., the army of Alexander the Great, based in present-day Greece, will use a combination of infantry (or foot soldiers) and cavalry (soldiers on horseback) to create an empire. Alexander's infantry advance toward the enemy, thrusting with their spears. Then his cavalry gallop into the fight on their horses. The cavalry's thundering charges will help Alexander win most of his battles.

Three centuries later, the Romans will have built an army of over 300,000 professional soldiers, many of them in infantry units called legions. To keep the men in a legion tough, all share in punishments. If a unit doesn't fight hard enough, every tenth man in the legion is killed.

Throughout ancient times, weapons grow more powerful and battles become more deadly. Your goal is simple: to stay alive.

THE RUSTED REMAINS of a Roman soldier's short, double-edged sword and its scabbard, or holder. A soldier would wear such a sword attached to his belt. This particular sword was made in the 300s A.D.

Tutankhamen

FOR CENTURIES IN ANCIENT TIMES, Egypt did not need to worry much about invading armies. Egypt was protected by two natural barriers, the Mediterranean Sea to the north and the vast deserts to the west and east of the Nile River. But as its neighbors became more powerful, Egypt formed a professional army.

By about 1250 B.C., this army has grown to include over 100,000 men. The pharaoh orders soldiers to join the army. Even a ten-year-old boy can find himself among the ranks. He will have to march for hours across the desert, choking on dust, suffering with thirst, and burned by the sun. Some officers wear armor. But ordinary soldiers fight in just a loincloth, a cloth worn around the waist. Soldiers carry spears, battle-axes, and shields made of wood and animal skins.

A pharaoh's army consists of foot soldiers, archers, and chariot drivers. Chariots are light and easy to maneuver. They usually carry two men: one driver and one archer. In battle they pick off enemy soldiers one by one until the rest are terrified and run away.

In this painting, the young pharaoh Tutankhamen is driving and fighting from his chariot. To leave his hands free to use his bow, he has tied the reins around his body.

Usually the pharaoh or his son commands the Egyptian army. But because Tutankhamen is only eighteen when he dies (in around 1332 B.C.), he probably never leads the army in war. That means this is an imaginary scene. Its purpose is to show Tutankhamen as a god who defeats his enemies. He is shown battling the Nubians, tribesmen from Africa, who lie dead in heaps, their bodies bristling with arrows.

TUTANKHAMEN IN HIS CHARIOT ATTACKING NUBIANS
PAINTED WOODEN CHEST, EGYPTIAN, *c.* 1332–1322 B.C., ARTISTS UNKNOWN

Tomb Treasure

The scene shown below and on the facing page is painted on the side of a wooden chest, one of the fabulous treasures found in Tutankhamen's tomb. The tomb is at the end of a narrow tunnel cut into a rocky hillside in Egypt's Valley of the Kings, the burial place for many ancient Egyptian pharaohs.

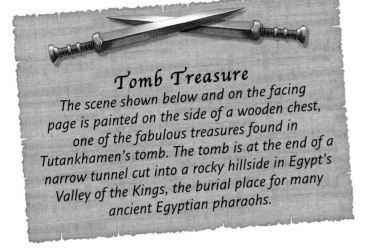

Shades for the pharaoh These fans are sunshades made from feathers. Attendants carry the shades in royal processions or at religious ceremonies but not in battle. The attendants may be Nubians, captured in a previous war and made into slaves. They may be included here to show Egypt's power to control the Nubian people.

Deadly weapon The most lethal Egyptian weapon is the composite bow, which can be used while riding in a chariot. It is made from layers of wood, animal tendon, and horn. These materials make it powerful enough to kill up to 200 yards (180 m) away—the length of two football fields.

Ammunition supply Tutankhamen carries a quiver, or case, that can hold 30 arrows. The arrows are made of reeds fitted with flint (hard stone) or bronze tips.

Terra-cotta Army

IN EARLIEST TIMES, CHINA CONSISTED OF A NUMBER OF STATES, which were always at war with each other. But in 221 B.C. they are united by Shi Huangdi, who calls himself the first Chinese emperor.

Shi's greatest achievement is to complete the Great Wall of China by linking sections of earlier walls. The Great Wall makes a continuous barrier over 1,000 miles (1,600 km) long. The wall protects Shi's empire from raiding tribes. But the emperor's rule is harsh. If you disagree with him, you are either beheaded, chopped in half, or boiled alive.

Shi Huangdi has a great fear of dying. When he was only thirteen years old, he ordered work to begin on his tomb. He wants to create a vast underground kingdom where he will rule after his death. It will be arranged like a great map of the earth, with rivers made of mercury and a roof studded with stars made of pearls. An army of soldiers all made from baked clay, or terra-cotta, will protect Emperor Shi in the afterlife. To prevent the tomb from being robbed, loaded crossbows will be set up to shoot intruders. This ghostly world will be lit by lamps burning walrus oil.

Although old documents studied by historians talked about this great tomb, it was not until 1974 that Chinese archaeologists began digging and the wonders of Shi's tomb were revealed. Archaeologists were astonished to discover a series of pits containing more than 6,000 life-sized statues. Made of terra-cotta, and drawn up in orderly ranks, this spectacular pottery army includes foot soldiers, kneeling archers, cavalrymen with their horses, and war chariots. It took 700,000 laborers to build the tomb. Those who knew its secrets were buried alive when the work was done.

TERRA-COTTA ARMY, XIAN, CHINA, c. 246–210 B.C., ARTISTS UNKNOWN

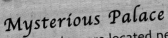

Mysterious Palace

The terra-cotta warriors are located near the city of Xian, in Shensi province, China. In 1974 archaeologists thought that investigating the tomb would take a week. But it is so big—more than 3 miles (5 km) across—that it has not all been studied yet. No one knows what is inside Shi's royal palace, which is still to be uncovered.

Missing weapons This kneeling warrior would have been holding a crossbow, but all the weapons buried in the tomb were stolen soon after the tomb was made. They were real weapons, so the robbers may have used them in battle.

Horse and rider This cavalryman stands at attention with his horse behind him. His short robe is ideal for riding. His tough little Mongolian horse will carry him for miles without tiring. The horse has a saddle, but no stirrups, since they have not yet been invented.

Handmade heads This warrior wears his hair twisted into a knot on his head. Every warrior in the tomb has a different face. Their heads were made one by one, not cast in standard molds. Traces of paint found on the figures and horses show that when they were buried they were all brightly colored. The paint has since worn away.

Alexander the Great

I T IS THE YEAR 334 B.C. ALEXANDER, THE YOUNG KING OF MACEDONIA, has left home at the head of a magnificent army. Alexander already controls the countries that make up modern Greece. He intends to conquer the Persians, in what is now Turkey. His aim is to free the Greek people living there from the tyranny of the mighty Persian empire. But soon he decides to go farther and overthrow the Persian king completely.

The main parts of Alexander's army are armored cavalrymen and infantrymen. The infantrymen fight in a tight square formation called a phalanx. Alexander's cavalry and infantry both use long spears: 12 feet (4 m) long for the cavalry, and up to 18 feet (6 m) or more for the infantry.

After marching his army a great distance, Alexander at last meets his enemy, Darius III, King of Persia, in the Battle of Issus. Darius is leading a huge army of 160,000 men, which outnumbers Alexander's by about four to one. Drawn up on the banks of a river, the Persians look unbeatable. But Alexander is a brave and clever leader in battle.

First, the infantrymen of the phalanx lower their spears and advance toward the enemy with a terrifying wall of steel. Then Alexander leads his cavalry in a charge across the river. Men and horses struggle across while spears crash. The air is thick with dust and flying arrows. Alexander, riding at the head of his cavalry, suddenly comes face to face with Darius in his chariot. Alexander is wounded in the thigh fighting with Darius's guards. But Darius, seeing that Alexander's army is winning the battle, turns and flees.

At the age of only twenty-three, Alexander has defeated Darius. In the next ten years, he will continue to win battles, creating a vast empire. No wonder he will come to be known as Alexander the Great.

A Million Little Pieces

This picture is a mosaic, made by sticking small pieces of colored material onto a surface. This mosaic is made from a million and a half tiny bits of colored stone. It is 2,200 years old and is thought to be a copy of an even older picture, a painting by Philossenos, a Greek artist who lived at the time of Alexander the Great. No one knows who designed the mosaic or who made it.

THE BATTLE OF ISSUS, FROM "THE ALEXANDER MOSAIC"
SECOND CENTURY B.C., ARTISTS UNKNOWN

Star quality With his curly hair and brown eyes, Alexander looks noble and handsome. But as far as we know, the real Alexander was short and stocky, with a big nose and small eyes. This image helps him look like his name, Alexander the Great.

Guards and friends Riding just behind Alexander is a special regiment of cavalry called the Companions. Alexander risks his life leading the Companions in an all-out charge at the Battle of Issus and in other battles.

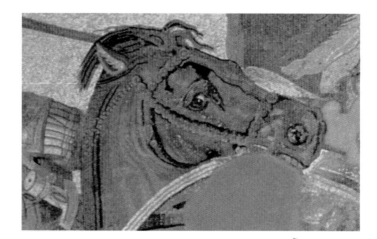

No ordinary horse Alexander's horse, named Bucephalus, carries him through many dangers. Fierce and high strung, Bucephalus allows no one but Alexander to ride him. Stories say that when the king wanted to mount the horse, Bucephalus knelt so that Alexander could step into the saddle.

Whip hand The royal chariot driver uses a whiplash to make the Persian troops move. Once he has cleared a path, he will drive King Darius away, escaping from Alexander's forces.

In the saddle This Persian cavalryman is wearing a soft cloth called a tiara on his head, which gives him little protection. He wears no body armor. Most of Alexander's soldiers wear helmets and breastplates and have much longer spears than the Persians. These are some of the reasons why they win the battle.

Runaway king Instead of leading his army into battle, Darius watches it from the rear. When Alexander confronts him, Darius panics and flees. He leaves his wife and children behind. They are captured by Alexander.

With the Roman Legion

Not far from Alexander the Great's home in Northern Greece, another empire is emerging. In 500 B.C., Rome is little more than a cluster of villages in what is now Italy. But 600 years later, the Romans have built the largest empire the world has ever seen. Within the empire, a Roman can travel thousands of miles on paved roads, from Mesopotamia (modern Iraq) to England.

But the sheer size of the Roman Empire is becoming a problem. It is difficult to patrol the frontiers, or borders. Outsiders, whom the Romans call "barbarians," frequently make attacks. Only a very large army can control the empire and its frontiers.

The Roman army is made up of legions, infantry units of about 5,000 men. Each legion is divided into centuries, or groups of 80 to 100 men. Six centuries make up a cohort, and ten cohorts a legion.

Members of a legion are called legionaries. Legionaries are well trained and well armed. They can march 20 miles (32 km) a day wearing armor and carrying weapons, tools, and other equipment.

In about 250 A.D., Roman legionaries meet barbarians in Northern Europe. This sculpture gives a detailed view of the battle. Most fighting is done at close quarters. As a legionary, you would brandish your sword and charge forward, cutting and thrusting at the enemy until one of you dies or is badly wounded. Here, legionaries grab barbarians by the hair or clothes. They trample them under their horses. In this battle, there are no rules of fair play: it is kill or be killed.

THE LUDOVISI BATTLE SARCOPHAGUS
c. 250 A.D., ARTISTS UNKNOWN

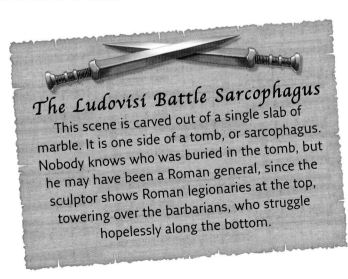

The Ludovisi Battle Sarcophagus

This scene is carved out of a single slab of marble. It is one side of a tomb, or sarcophagus. Nobody knows who was buried in the tomb, but he may have been a Roman general, since the sculptor shows Roman legionaries at the top, towering over the barbarians, who struggle hopelessly along the bottom.

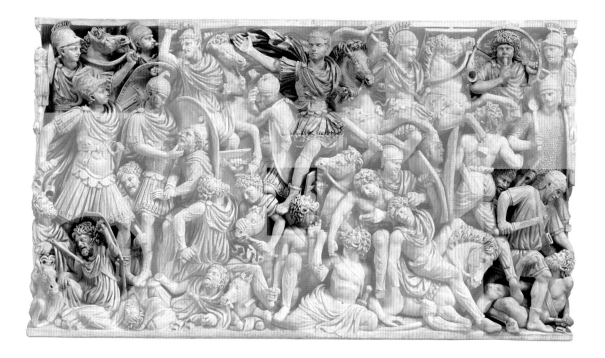

S *turdy shoes*
Legionaries wear leather sandals called caligae. The soles are made of several layers of leather stuck together and fitted with iron studs. The sandals are so tough that many have survived from Roman times.

C *ut and thrust* This legionary is about to kill a barbarian with a short stabbing sword called a gladius. It is an ideal weapon for hand-to-hand fighting. The legionary is wearing a helmet but seems to have lost his shield during the battle.

S *udden death* This barbarian has been stabbed through the heart and is dying. His thick curly hair, mustache, and beard make him easy to distinguish from the clean-shaven Roman legionaries.

Bugle blast Trumpets and horns (called cornus) were used in the Roman army to sound the alarm when danger approached. Since they could be heard above the noise of battle, they were also used to send orders to the soldiers.

A good job? Joining the legion is considered a good career for a young man, but life for a legionary isn't easy. These young Roman soldiers remain in the army for 25 years and are not allowed to marry during that time. Although their training is tough and discipline strict, they are well paid and well fed.

Victory salute Astride his rearing horse, a young Roman general raises his arm to encourage his troops. He is wearing metal armor over his woolen tunic. Because he is fighting in the colder climate of Northern Europe, he has a woolen cloak tied around his shoulders.

The Age of Armor

THE AGE OF KNIGHTS AND CASTLES BEGAN MORE THAN 1,000 YEARS AGO. EUROPE WAS JUST ENTERING A TIME KNOWN AS THE MIDDLE AGES WHEN THE FIRST KNIGHTS RODE OFF TO BATTLE AND ADVENTURE.

PICTURE THIS: IT IS OCTOBER 15, 1066. YOU ARE A YOUNG FOOT SOLDIER in the army of Duke William of Normandy. You are on a battlefield near a town in southern England called Hastings and you are exhausted after fighting and winning a great battle the day before.

Many of your friends have been killed or wounded. But far more men from the English army are dead. You have heard that the English king and two of his brothers were cut down during the fighting.

You know that your army's victory was inspired by Duke William's leadership. He was probably just as nervous as you were before the fighting started. In fact, a story is going around that he put on his chain-mail armor—a suit of interlocking metal rings—back to front to start with and had to make a joke about it. But after that, he was always in the thick of the fight, inspiring everyone through the long hours of combat.

CROSSBOWS, LIKE THIS ONE, were the most powerful war bows ever made. Their lethal bolts can pierce through any armor, but they take a long time to reload. Crossbowmen usually fight beside other troops, who protect them while they are reloading.

Now you are searching the battlefield for arrows for your bow. You fired almost all of those you had yesterday and need to find some replacements. You see the bodies of many English soldiers, most of them wearing only their ordinary clothes. They were easy targets for you and your friends. You don't wear armor either, but richer men on both sides have chain mail like Duke William's. If you're lucky, you can get some for yourself by taking it from one of the dead bodies.

All the soldiers in the English army yesterday did their fighting on foot—no match for the armored knights on horseback in your army. You can't know it, but over the coming centuries, knights will continually improve their defenses. Chain mail will be replaced by heavier armor made of solid metal plates. They will ride warhorses called *destriers*, specially bred to carry the weight of an armored knight. The horses will wear armor too. The impact of a charging knight on his big heavy horse is like being hit by a small car. Throughout the 1100s and 1200s, armored knights will be Europe's most fearsome and powerful soldiers.

But eventually armored knights will fall to even more powerful weapons: longbows, a specialty of the English army, and crossbows. By the 1300s crossbows have been developed with the power to fire an iron bolt through plate armor. They are used by many countries' armies. At the Battle of Crécy, France, in 1346, hundreds of French knights are killed by English archers who let loose a tremendous hail of arrows from their longbows. Although their arrows seldom pierce steel plates, they can find chinks where the plates join. They can certainly kill or wound a knight's lighter-armored horse.

Highly disciplined foot soldiers armed with long spears called pikes, or halberds—like a pike and ax combined—can also stop a cavalry charge dead in its tracks. Horses won't charge toward a bristling wall of spear points, if the men holding the spears stand firm and don't run away.

When gunpowder is brought to Europe from China in the 1300s, the days of the armored knight—once the terror of the European battlefield—are numbered. Even the knights' castles are taking a beating.

THIS ELEPHANT'S COAT of chain mail will protect it from spears and arrows. It was made in India in the 1600s. Armies used elephants in battle as long ago as the time of Alexander the Great. The elephants carried armed warriors and also terrified the enemy's horses.

AT A HEIGHT OF 6 FEET 8 INCHES (2.06 m), this is the tallest suit of armor in the world. It was made in Germany in about 1540. Although a boy might start military training from the age of seven, the small suit of armor beside the larger one was probably a gift for a younger boy.

Early castles in Europe were simple wooden towers built on high mounds of earth. As the age of armor progresses, wooden towers and walls are replaced by higher stone walls, which offer better protection to the people inside. But even these massive stone walls can't hold out against the cannons that armies use from the 1400s.

In 1453, during the Battle of Castillon, French forces mow down armored English cavalry with cannons.

This is the first time these weapons play a decisive part in an open battle. From now on, archers and knights will no longer dominate battles. Big guns and gunners are taking their place.

Norman Conquerors

LONG AFTER THE END OF THE ROMAN EMPIRE, A GREAT BATTLE IS TAKING SHAPE IN ENGLAND. Called the Battle of Hastings, it is recorded in a long embroidered cloth (now known as the Bayeux Tapestry), a few years after the fighting ends. The tapestry tells the story of the battle and events leading up to it.

Harold Godwinson, the most powerful lord in England, has promised to help William, Duke of Normandy (part of what is now France), become king of England after the death of the current king, Edward. But instead, when the time comes, Harold proclaims himself king. Enraged by this betrayal, William sails from Normandy to England with an army of 7,000 men. Landing on England's south coast, near the town of Hastings, William marches to meet King Harold's army.

Early on October 14, 1066, the Battle of Hastings begins. Duke William orders his archers to attack, launching arrows from their bows. But the hail of hissing arrows can't get past the shields, which the English are holding together to form a kind of shield-wall. Then, William sends in his infantry. They, too, are pushed back.

In the scene in the tapestry above, the English are desperately defending themselves behind their shield-wall. The violence of the battle spills over into the tapestry's

THE BAYEUX TAPESTRY
PROBABLY 1073–1083
ARTISTS UNKNOWN

The Bayeux Tapestry

This tapestry is over 900 years old. It is made with colored wool embroidered onto a strip of linen 230 feet (70 m) long and 20 inches (50 cm) high. It contains 626 human figures, 190 horses, 35 dogs, and other animals, as well as trees, ships, and buildings. It was probably made by craftswomen in a monastery in Canterbury, England. It is now on display in the town of Bayeux, France, from which it gets its name.

lower border, where men lie dead and dying amid broken swords and abandoned shields.

As the battle continues, the Norman attackers begin to panic. Soon, soldiers are spreading a rumor that their leader, Duke William, has been killed. When William hears of the rumor, he takes off his helmet to show his face. Then, protected only by his suit of chain-mail armor, he leads a ferocious cavalry charge. Horses rear, throwing riders. Swords and lances flash and strike. Screams of pain fill the air. With a combined attack of cavalry and infantry, William at last defeats the English. Harold is killed and William becomes the new king of England.

Battle-ax *This fearsome ax is so heavy that the English soldier needs two hands to use it. He is about to bring it crashing down on a horse. With its curved blade and great weight, a battle-ax can slice through a horse's head.*

Wooden wall *These soldiers' kite-shaped shields are probably made of wood covered with leather. Standing close together, the English soldiers overlap their shields so that they form a wall to protect their bodies. Some Norman arrows have stuck into the shields, but none have pierced them.*

Mane attraction It is easy to tell that this is a Norman cavalryman because his horse has a long flowing mane. The English horses in the tapestry are shown with their manes cut very short.

Knock out The mace is a powerful clublike weapon with a spiked and knobby iron head attached to a wooden handle. Soldiers generally use a mace as they use a club, but sometimes they throw it. This mace flies through the air, aimed at a charging Norman cavalryman.

Desperate defense An English archer aims and fires his bow as quickly as he can to try to drive back the ferocious Norman cavalry charge.

Tall in the saddle This Norman cavalryman's stirrups help him stay in the saddle when he is using his weapons. Imagine how difficult this would have been before stirrups were invented to help riders control their horses. Stirrups first came to the West from central Asia in around the ninth century.

Dressed to kill While most soldiers wear ordinary clothing, nearly every soldier shown in the tapestry is wearing chain mail, flexible armor made from interlocking metal rings. A soldier pulls his chain-mail tunic over his head and ties it at his knees. Armor gives soldiers much protection. But it cannot guard against every arrow tip or blow from a battle-ax, as this soldier has discovered.

Religious Wars

IT IS THE LATE SUMMER OF 1096. YOU ARE A YOUNG AND RICH NOBLEMAN IN EUROPE, WITH A LARGE ESTATE. Your life is peaceful, but you are going to give it all up to join other European Christians to form an army. This army will journey some 2,400 miles (3,800 km) to fight Muslims for control of the Holy Land, a region in the Middle East that has religious importance to Christians, Muslims, and Jews.

Your struggle to bring the Holy Land under Christian control will be called a Crusade. The word Crusade comes from the Latin word for cross, and you will wear a cross sewn onto your clothes. The Crusade will be very expensive. You have to buy horses, armor, weapons, wagons, and food. You may be away for years. But you are going because you believe you are fighting for God.

You cannot know that your Crusade—with its many battles—will be the first of many, or that the Crusades will last for more than 200 years. Towns will be destroyed. Their populations—including women and children—will be massacred. Thousands of people will be killed in battle. Both Christian and Muslim soldiers will do terrible things during the Crusades.

What is the result of your Crusade and the others that follow? After so many years of death and destruction, by the late 1200s the Christians will lose control of the Holy Land to the Muslims.

In this picture, Christian knights are riding their high-stepping horses into battle. The Muslim forces, which include warriors from many parts of the Middle East, are preparing to meet the charge.

CHRISTIANS FIGHTING MUSLIMS
SONGBOOK, MADE FOR KING ALFONSO OF CASTILE AND LEON, 1200s, ARTISTS UNKNOWN

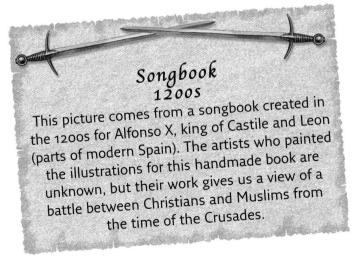

Songbook
1200s
This picture comes from a songbook created in the 1200s for Alfonso X, king of Castile and Leon (parts of modern Spain). The artists who painted the illustrations for this handmade book are unknown, but their work gives us a view of a battle between Christians and Muslims from the time of the Crusades.

K **nights ready for battle** This knight is riding in a tall saddle with his legs almost straight in the stirrups. This gives him a steady seat so he can use his weapons effectively. It is not so good for guiding his large and clumsy horse. The Muslim warriors have lighter equipment and more nimble horses. They will try to outmaneuver the Christians.

H **eavy armor** This German helmet is one of the types worn by Crusaders. Made of steel, it is padded inside to make it more comfortable, but it is very heavy. When the fighting takes place in hot countries like Syria and Lebanon, the helmet will become stifling inside.

S **ymbols of faith** The crescent moon is the emblem of the Muslim faith. The artist has painted moons on this warrior's shield to show that he is a Muslim.

Cavalry charge *Christian knights wear padded jackets over their chain mail. They ride their horses in close-packed formation and charge the enemy with their lances lowered. The Muslims rely on their horses' speed to dodge the Crusaders' charge.*

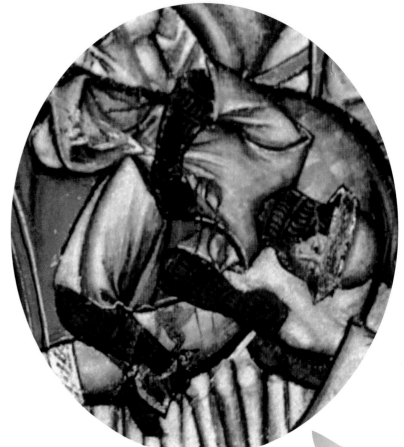

Powerful mounts *This horse is protected by a thick padded cloth. It has been trained to charge enemy troops and is able to carry a man wearing heavy armor. There are no horses like this one bred in the Middle East. Arab horses are small and speedy.*

Casualties in battle *This Muslim warrior is badly hurt. Doctors in the Middle East are more skillful than European doctors, so the warrior may recover from his wounds. If he is captured by the Crusaders and survives, he will probably be exchanged for a Christian prisoner or sold back to the Muslim army.*

The Battle of Crécy

ON AUGUST 26, 1346, ON A HILL NEAR THE VILLAGE OF CRÉCY IN NORTHERN FRANCE, the English King Edward III comes face to face with the French army—which is nearly three times larger than his own. Edward has announced his claim to the French throne. Capturing that throne will prove to be a harder task than Edward hopes. The Battle of Crécy is the first major battle in what will become known as the Hundred Years' War between England and France.

The battle begins with the French marching toward the English. The first to advance are the French crossbowmen, who carry short bows mounted at the end of wooden stocks and operated by cranks. But, before the crossbowmen have time to fire, English longbowmen cut them down with a hail of arrows.

French cavalry follow after the crossbowmen. As they struggle to advance up the muddy hillside on horseback, they are massacred by English archers. Horses, driven wild with pain and fear, crash to the ground, throwing their riders. The English rush in to stab or club to death many of the fallen knights in the French cavalry.

At dawn the next day, mounds of dead and dying men and horses lie in the battlefield around the English army. The French have lost over 1,500 men. The English have lost fewer than 100.

In this scene from an illustrated book completed some time after the battle, English longbowmen are taking aim while most of the French army retreats toward a castle. The scene appears calm. It shows none of the real horrors of the battle.

THE BATTLE OF CRÉCY
ILLUMINATED MANUSCRIPT, FRENCH, 1400s
ARTISTS UNKNOWN

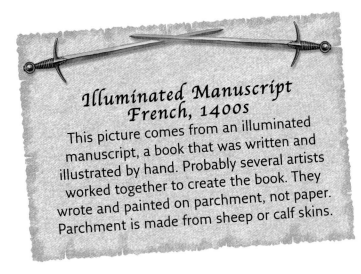

Illuminated Manuscript French, 1400s

This picture comes from an illuminated manuscript, a book that was written and illustrated by hand. Probably several artists worked together to create the book. They wrote and painted on parchment, not paper. Parchment is made from sheep or calf skins.

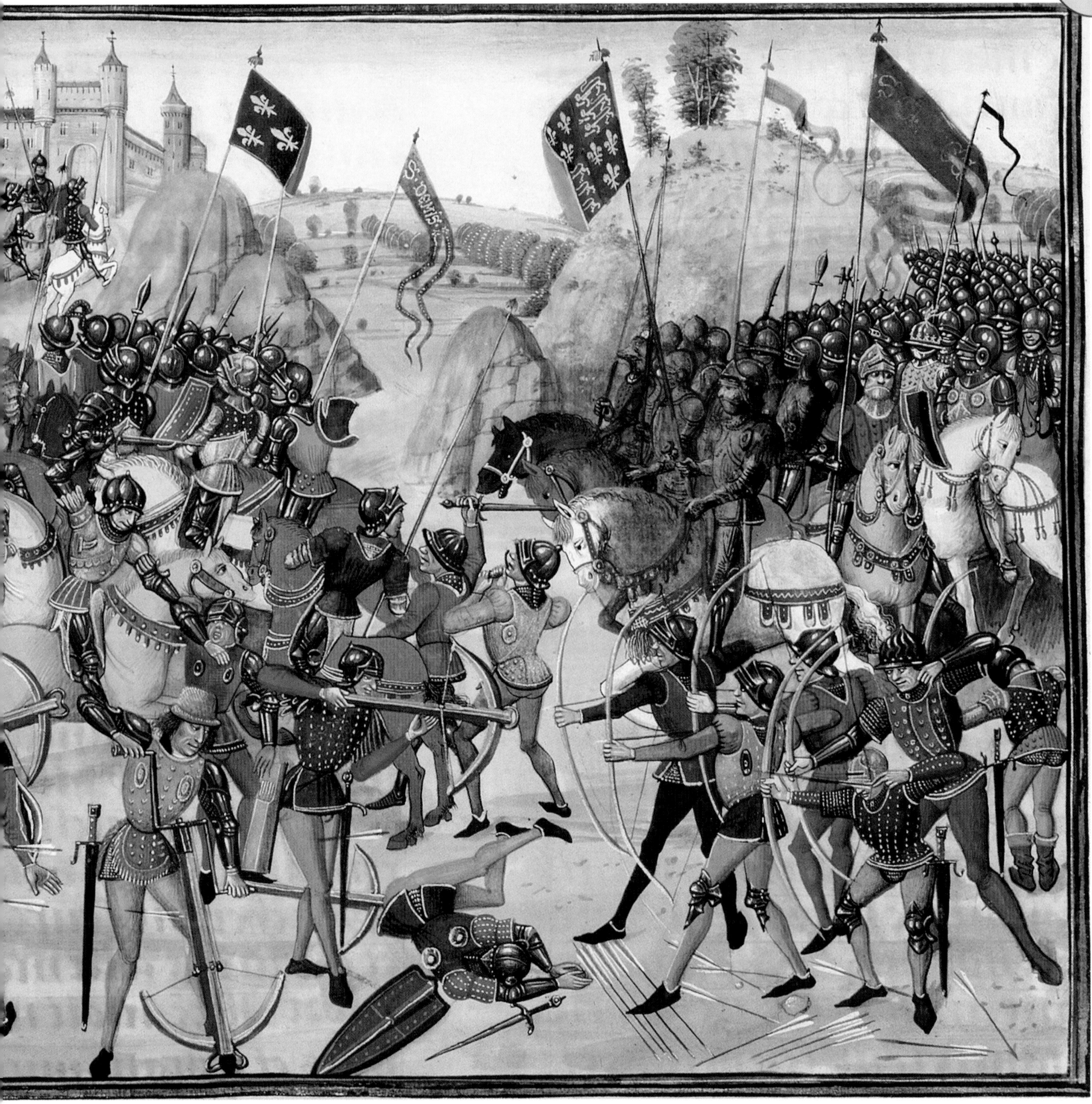

C **rank it up** This French soldier is reloading his crossbow. Turning the crank takes precious seconds, much longer than it takes to reload an English longbow, which has no crank. This means the French soldier is under constant fire from the enemy. He already has one English arrow in his thigh.

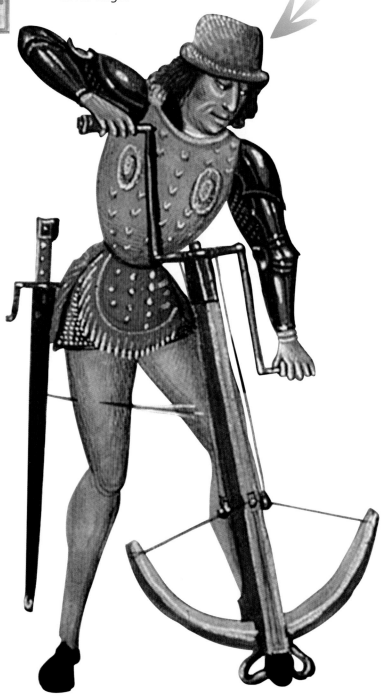

I **maginary castle** There was no castle near the battlefield at Crécy, but the artist included an imaginary one. With its towers and pointed roofs, it looks like several other castles, or châteaux, in France. Some of the knights who fought at Crécy lived in grand castles like this one.

Great balls of fire Cannons were not used at Crécy, but a year later King Edward III used them in another battle. The little bird is a mystery, since birds would be frightened off by cannon fire. It may be a private joke between the artist and the person who paid for the manuscript. Or the artist may have dropped ink on the page and disguised the mistake by turning it into a bird.

Deadly enemies English archers go through years of training before they can use a longbow well. They have to be strong enough to bend their bows back a long way if their arrows are to fly powerfully through the air. They are so feared and hated by the French that if an archer is captured alive, the French cut two fingers off his right hand so that he can never shoot his bow again.

Slashed sleeve This English soldier (at lower right) has raised his arm in a desperate attempt to protect himself. But the French knight on horseback has grabbed it, and is about to bring his sword crashing down. Double-edged swords like this one can be used either to stab or to slash.

Guns and Cannons

FROM 1400 TO THE 1800S, HANDGUNS AND ARTILLERY WEAPONS BECOME MORE POWERFUL. GOVERNMENTS TRAIN MUCH BIGGER AND MORE EFFICIENT ARMIES. WARS ARE MORE TERRIBLE THAN EVER BEFORE.

PICTURE THIS: IT IS THE YEAR 1777. You are a soldier in the American colonies. You are being attacked by the British during one of the battles of the Revolutionary War.

This is your first battle. The noise of musket and artillery fire is deafening, and you are blinded by gunpowder smoke. You are desperately trying to load your musket, a heavy gun fired from the shoulder. The British Redcoats are advancing. You are frightened but there is not a moment to lose.

First grab a cartridge—a paper tube holding enough gunpowder for one shot and a single lead ball. You must bite off the end of the cartridge and put a little of the gunpowder into the firing mechanism of the gun. Then you force the rest of the powder, the ball, and paper into the end of the barrel. Ram all this firmly down the barrel with your ramrod (a thin metal pole kept in a holder underneath the barrel). Don't forget to take your ramrod out again. Now you are ready to aim and fire! With practice, you should be able to fire two or even three shots in a minute. If you are a good shot, you might hit an enemy 50 yards (46 m) away.

MONSTER GUN *This massive 6-ton cannon was made around 1450 and was used by King James II of Scotland to smash enemy castles. Its cannonballs weigh more than 330 pounds (150 kg). It is known as Mons Meg and is on display at Edinburgh Castle in Scotland.*

SIX-SHOOTER *This is a Colt revolver. It can fire more than once before it must be reloaded. Six bullets are loaded into a cylinder that revolves when you pull the trigger. When the cylinder revolves, a new bullet is ready to be fired. The Colt revolver was invented in 1835 by an American, Samuel Colt.*

Although it takes a long time to load a musket, yours is a much better weapon than soldiers had in the 1600s. In those days, guns quite often blew up in a soldier's face. Older weapons were also so heavy that you had to prop them up on a forked stick before you could aim and fire.

Muskets are not the only weapons of your day to use gunpowder. The explosive is also used to fire cannons. Many early cannons in the 1400s were large and heavy. One used in Turkey required 16 oxen and 200 men to move it. Loaded with a huge stone ball weighing 1,000 pounds (500 kg), it could be fired only seven times in a day!

Later in the 1400s cannons were smaller and lighter. Each one could be towed by a team of about six horses. In 1521, a Spaniard named Hernán Cortés used 10 cannons and 600 men to conquer the mighty Aztec empire of what is now Mexico.

Cannons also played a vital role in battles at sea. In 1588, an English fleet of some 170 sailing ships, armed with about 1,800 cannons, defeated a Spanish invasion fleet in the English Channel. During the war in which you are fighting, the largest warships have crews of 1,000 men and are each armed with more than 100 cannons.

By 1800, all the big European countries have permanent armies of soldiers who are paid by the government. Armies are divided into groups called regiments. Soldiers are highly trained so that they can maneuver in formation on the battlefield. They halt to fire, reload, then march forward again.

Their goal is to act as one large gun, moving and shooting together. Guns and cannons transform warfare. But battles and weapons will become even more sophisticated—and deadly—in centuries to come.

FLINTLOCK *This flintlock musket was made in Germany in 1646. The firing mechanism (or lock) uses a flint (stone) to strike sparks from a piece of metal. This ignites the gunpowder and fires the gun. The flintlock doesn't always work, especially if it is raining.*

The American Revolution

I
T IS JUNE 1775. PEOPLE LIVING IN THE THIRTEEN AMERICAN
COLONIES ARE TIRED OF BEING RULED BY THE BRITISH. The British
government is trying to introduce new taxes and change laws in
the colonies. Colonists have not been consulted about these changes.
Simmering anger at this unfair situation is boiling over into war. Many
Americans are ready to fight for their independence from Britain in
what will become known as the Revolutionary War.

Boston, in Massachusetts, is occupied by British soldiers. Overlooking
the town are two hills, Breed's Hill and Bunker Hill. At dawn on June
17, 1775, the British are astonished to see that overnight the hills have
been occupied by American troops. Some 2,300 British set out to drive
the colonists away.

Attaching their bayonets (dagger-like blades) to their guns, the red-
coated British soldiers march steadily and silently uphill. The colonists
wait until the enemy is very close, then let loose a crushing volley of
musket fire. Many Redcoats fall dead or wounded. The survivors retreat
in confusion.

But again the British attack. Again they are driven back. On the third
attack, they manage to reach the American positions. Men die on both
sides as the soldiers club each other with their muskets and stab with
their swords and bayonets. The colonists are forced to retreat. But the
British have lost twice as many men. This battle—called the Battle of
Bunker Hill—is the first major combat of the American Revolution. It
proves to the colonists that they can stand up to the British and gives
them hope that they might one day defeat them.

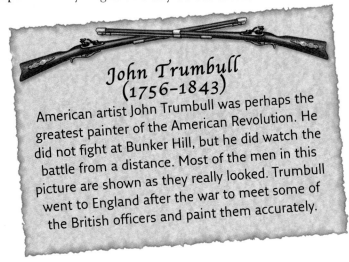

John Trumbull
(1756–1843)

American artist John Trumbull was perhaps the
greatest painter of the American Revolution. He
did not fight at Bunker Hill, but he did watch the
battle from a distance. Most of the men in this
picture are shown as they really looked. Trumbull
went to England after the war to meet some of
the British officers and paint them accurately.

THE BATTLE OF BUNKER (OR BUNKER'S) HILL, 1786
JOHN TRUMBULL

Dying general General Joseph Warren of the colonial forces lies dying after being shot in the final British attack of the battle. Although Warren is the senior American officer, Colonel William Prescott is the main American commander. He tells his men, "Don't shoot until you see the whites of their eyes."

Flags flying When the Battle of Bunker Hill is fought, the United States does not yet exist. Neither does the American flag, with its familiar stars and stripes. During the Revolutionary War American forces use a wide variety of flags in battle. This flag (below, left) is from Massachusetts. Men from Massachusetts and Connecticut make up a large part of the American force at Bunker Hill.

Rally round the flag Until the late 1800s, army units in all countries often carry flags into combat. This helps their soldiers to know where to form up and fight amid the noise and chaos of a battle. This flag (near right) is a British regimental flag.

Family tragedy Major John Pitcairn of the British Marines (center) has been shot at Bunker Hill and will die shortly afterward. His son, Lieutenant William Pitcairn (right) is trying to help his father. Many of the British attackers are cut down by the deadly American musket fire.

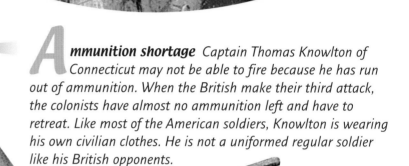

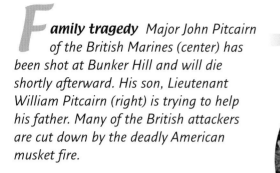

Ammunition shortage Captain Thomas Knowlton of Connecticut may not be able to fire because he has run out of ammunition. When the British make their third attack, the colonists have almost no ammunition left and have to retreat. Like most of the American soldiers, Knowlton is wearing his own civilian clothes. He is not a uniformed regular soldier like his British opponents.

With sword and musket Lieutenant Thomas Grosvenor of the Connecticut forces, one of the first to open fire on the British, has been wounded in the hand. Behind him, his servant Asaba is loading his gun. Asaba is one of more than 100 blacks who fight with the colonists at Bunker Hill.

The French Revolution

I T IS 1789. IN PARIS, FRANCE, people gather in the streets and cafés. They are angry and restless. Life is unfair: the rich seem to get richer, and the poor get poorer. Now there is a shortage of bread. Everyone blames King Louis XVI and his government.

In the suburbs of Paris, there is a great prison fortress called the Bastille. People hear stories of hundreds of prisoners lying in the Bastille's dungeons. The stories grow until the Bastille becomes a symbol of everything people hate about the king and his rule.

Early on July 14, crowds that have been roaming the city of Paris begin to march to the Bastille. They are armed with weapons stolen from shops and from the king's storehouses. A mob of some 900 people, including one boy of only eight, gathers outside the prison.

The Bastille is guarded by only a handful of men, but they are well armed. The mob tries to force the governor of the prison to surrender. But when negotiations break down, the crowd grows impatient. In the confusion, someone fires shots. Soon a battle is raging. The mob tries to storm the Bastille, attacking in a great hail of stones and gunfire.

Knowing he does not have enough supplies to last through a long attack, the prison governor finally surrenders. The people rush in. Once inside the prison walls, they make a surprising discovery: only seven prisoners are in the cells.

The storming of the Bastille is the beginning of a revolution. By the end of the French Revolution, the king will be toppled from his throne, a new form of government called a republic will be put in place, and thousands will have died in street battles.

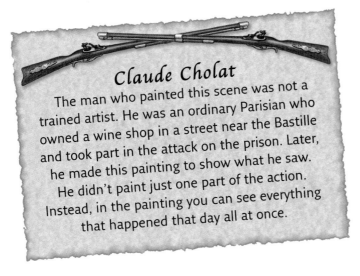

Claude Cholat

The man who painted this scene was not a trained artist. He was an ordinary Parisian who owned a wine shop in a street near the Bastille and took part in the attack on the prison. Later, he made this painting to show what he saw. He didn't paint just one part of the action. Instead, in the painting you can see everything that happened that day all at once.

THE STORMING OF THE BASTILLE, 1789
LIEUTENANT CLAUDE CHOLAT

des Vainqueur de la Bastille   Siege de la Bastille

Bag o'nails Many men in the crowd are armed with muskets. Although the artist shows much gunfire, many of the attackers have no gunpowder and cannot fire. Others have gunpowder but no shot, or bullets. One man buys nails from a store and loads them into his musket on the way to the Bastille.

A sorry end One of the defenders is killed and falls from the battlements of the Bastille. Historians disagree about the number of dead. But it is certain that the attackers fare far worse than the guards: about 100 attackers die and over 70 are wounded during the assault. The prison governor is killed after he surrenders the Bastille. The mob sticks his head on a spear and carries it through the streets of Paris.

Danger–falling objects The governor has ordered the firing positions of the prison to be widened so that his soldiers can shoot in all directions. He has also instructed his men to collect objects like paving stones and bits of iron to drop onto the head of anyone trying to climb the walls.

Stolen cannon This is one of the cannons taken by the mob on its way to the Bastille. They are unarmed, so they have stolen weapons from the king's storehouses to use in their attack. One of the attackers lies dead or wounded beside the cannon.

Tall tower The Bastille was built as a fortress, but used as a prison. At the time of the revolution, it has eight round towers, each with walls 5 feet (1.5 m) thick. In his painting, Cholat has exaggerated the height of the towers, making the prison look even larger than it really was.

Switching sides Before the mob storms the Bastille, the king sends in troops. But some royal troops, including this officer, are in sympathy with the mob. They join in when the Bastille is stormed. This officer is shown giving orders to some of the other attackers.

Sea Battle

NO WONDER THE BOY LOOKS AFRAID: on the horizon, just visible below a thunderous sky, is an enemy ship under full sail. Will it attack? The captain—on the right with the telescope—certainly thinks so. He is giving orders to prepare for action. The gun crews are already kneeling at their cannons. The ship's battle flag is about to be hauled up the mast.

Some of the ship's crew will not survive the battle. Yet, despite the fear and danger, they are excited to be going into action. They have been on the ship for months, living crammed together in the lower decks. They are used to the smell of unwashed bodies, the damp and the dark, the rats in the hold, and the bugs in the hard bread they eat. They are beaten if they don't obey orders. They have to work all the time to sail the ship and keep it ready for battle.

The two battling ships will probably hold their fire until they are within close range. Each ship will try to position itself so all its guns along one side can fire together. This is called a broadside. The shot hurtles along the enemy decks, smashing everything. Men are cut in half. Flying splinters of wood a foot (30 cm) or more long cause terrible wounds. A single broadside fired into the stern of an enemy ship can kill a hundred or more men, wreck the ship, and win the battle.

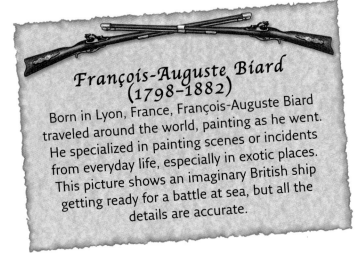

François-Auguste Biard (1798–1882)

Born in Lyon, France, François-Auguste Biard traveled around the world, painting as he went. He specialized in painting scenes or incidents from everyday life, especially in exotic places. This picture shows an imaginary British ship getting ready for a battle at sea, but all the details are accurate.

ON THE DECK DURING A SEA BATTLE, 1855
FRANÇOIS-AUGUSTE BIARD

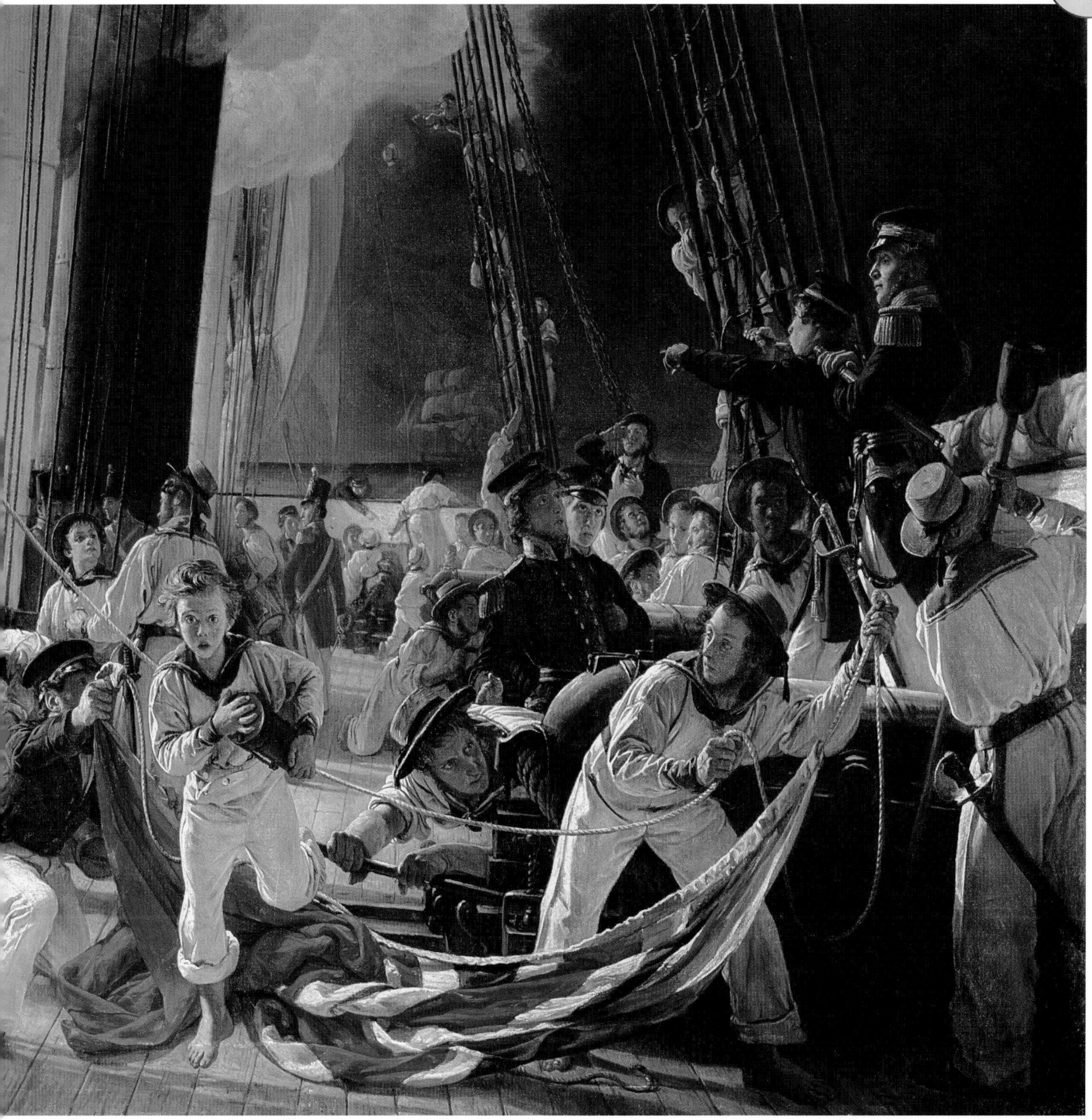

Young commanders These young men are midshipmen. They are the lowest ranking officers in the ship. Some may be as young as twelve. Like the other officers, they help to control the crew. During a battle, they may be put in charge of some of the guns, or cannons.

Soldiers and sailors Most warship crews include a group of soldiers called marines. They play only a small part in sailing the ship and do not operate any of the main cannons. Instead, in a battle, they fire their rifles at the enemy. If the ships get close enough, they will lead boarding parties onto the enemy vessel.

Protective barrier Most sailors sleep in hammocks—hanging beds. When the ship is being prepared for battle, crew members roll up their hammocks to make a padded wall called a breastwork. It helps protect the crew from enemy rifle fire. But a cannonball will blast straight through it.

Big guns When they are ready to fire, the gunners will run this cannon forward on its metal rails so that the muzzle pokes through the gunport—the firing hole in the ship's side. When it is fired, the cannon will recoil—jerk quickly backwards—and crush anyone who hasn't gotten out of the way. The noise is so loud that many gunners go deaf.

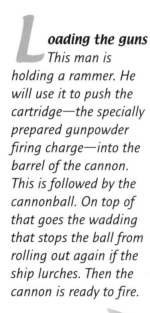

Loading the guns This man is holding a rammer. He will use it to push the cartridge—the specially prepared gunpowder firing charge—into the barrel of the cannon. This is followed by the cannonball. On top of that goes the wadding that stops the ball from rolling out again if the ship lurches. Then the cannon is ready to fire.

Dangerous duty This boy is called a powder monkey. He has collected gunpowder from the magazine—a special storeroom deep inside the ship—and is rushing it to a gun crew. Gunpowder is dangerous. The boy carries it in a metal box to protect it. If gunpowder comes in contact with a stray spark, it will explode. The boy's bare feet make it easier to run if the deck is awash with blood or seawater.

Reno's Retreat

IT IS JUNE 25, 1876, AND THE BATTLE OF LITTLE BIGHORN IS RAGING. U.S. Army soldiers and a large force of Plains Indians are fighting. Both Indians and U.S. soldiers are mounted on horseback. All are armed with guns, while some of the Indians also use bows and arrows.

Each group wants to control land in what is now South Dakota. The Black Hills of South Dakota are sacred to the Lakota Indians, sometimes called Sioux. According to treaties between the U.S. government and the Indians, whites are supposed to keep out of the area. But after a U.S. Army expedition led by General George Custer finds gold in the area, white miners flock to the Black Hills.

Soon thousands of Lakota and other Plains Indian warriors join together in a huge army. By June of 1876, they are camped near the Little Bighorn River in eastern Montana Territory.

U.S. Cavalry units, not realizing how large the Indian army is, split into groups to attack. General Custer and about 200 men from the 7th Cavalry Regiment are surrounded. All are killed. Major Marcus Reno, who leads another group of cavalry nearby, is forced to flee the battlefield. This part of the action is shown here in the picture, drawn by Amos Bad Heart Bull, an Oglala Lakota who grows up hearing many stories about the battle.

The Battle of Little Bighorn is a major victory for the Lakota. But the Lakota's long struggle over ancestral lands ends in 1890, when some 300 Indians are massacred at the Battle of Wounded Knee.

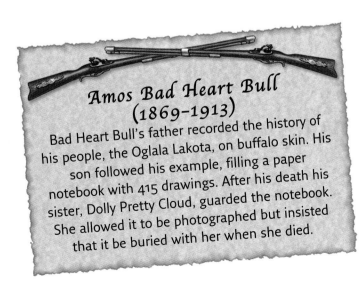

Amos Bad Heart Bull
(1869–1913)
Bad Heart Bull's father recorded the history of his people, the Oglala Lakota, on buffalo skin. His son followed his example, filling a paper notebook with 415 drawings. After his death his sister, Dolly Pretty Cloud, guarded the notebook. She allowed it to be photographed but insisted that it be buried with her when she died.

RETREAT OF MAJOR MARCUS RENO'S COMMAND, c.1900
AMOS BAD HEART BULL

Signs of bravery The Plains Indians wear war bonnets with eagle feathers because they believe the eagle is the greatest and most powerful of all birds. You could only wear an eagle feather if you had been awarded it by leaders of your tribe for being brave in battle.

Old-fashioned weapons The artist has shown this soldier with a sword at his side, but this is not correct. By this date, American cavalrymen took only guns with them into battle. Swords were not much good when your enemy avoided getting close to you but shot at you from a distance.

Prizes of battle When horses first came to America in the 1500s, they changed the way of life for Plains Indians forever. Ideal for hunting bison, horses became prized possessions and symbols of wealth and power. Here, a Lakota warrior has stopped fighting to guard the two horses he has captured.

New weapons For centuries Native Americans have used the bow and arrow, lance, and tomahawk. But white settlers and traders bring guns to the West. Some sell them to the Indians. At Little Bighorn, some Lakota use Winchester repeating rifles.

Shooting and missing This soldier is frantically trying to shoot at the Lakota warrior chasing him. At the same time, he rides his horse quickly to safety. Shooting accurately while riding a fast-moving horse is virtually impossible, so it is unlikely he will hit his enemy.

Modern Warfare

From the mid-1800s to the present, nations have used all their resources to defeat their enemies. Weapons are more deadly, bringing death and destruction on a huge scale.

Picture this! It is December 1862. You are only thirteen years old, but you are in the middle of a fierce battle. You are a drummer boy in the Seventh Michigan, a regiment in the Union Army. Your army is crossing the Rappahannock River in small boats to attack the town of Fredericksburg, Virginia. But the Confederates—the enemy—are firing at you.

The bullets fly thick and fast. Some of your comrades are dead. But you keep beating your drum to signal "No retreat!" The sound helps everyone keep going, despite their fear.

You are taking part in one of the battles of the American Civil War. The war began in 1861 and will last until 1865. It is considered the first "modern" war.

In the Civil War, new ways of fighting are developed. For the first time in war, railroads play a big part, carrying soldiers and supplies to the battlefields. Commanders communicate quickly over long distances by electric telegraph. At sea, a battle is fought between two ships driven by steam power instead of cloth sails.

A nation's military power now depends on its ability to use all of its people and all of its resources—science and industry, transportation, and communications—to prepare for and fight wars.

By the time of World War I (1914–1918), artillery weapons (developed from the cannons of earlier times) dominate the battlefields and cause most of the war's deaths. Artillery guns fire millions of shells, blasting everything in their path, killing thousands and turning battlefields

BULLET AFTER BULLET This Gatling gun can fire 400 bullets per minute. Guns like it were used in the Civil War. The gun's inventor, Richard Gatling, was a peace-loving man. He thought the gun was so frightening that it would stop countries from going to war.

CLOSE-RANGE FIREPOWER This is a Thompson submachine gun, used by the U.S. Army during World War II. It fires quick bursts of bullets but is only accurate at short range.

into huge swamps where some soldiers die from drowning in the mud.

War also becomes more cruel. By the end of World War I, every army is using chemical weapons, such as poison gas. At sea, submarines sink ships carrying food and supplies, not just for the armies but for civilians too. For the first time ever, aircraft are used in war on a large scale. They can bomb places miles behind the front lines. If you are a bomber pilot, it is possible to destroy towns and kill thousands of people you will never see.

World War II (1939–1945) is fought with much the same weapons as World War I. But these weapons have grown even more powerful. Entire cities and their populations are destroyed by bombs dropped by endless waves of aircraft. Great fleets of tanks (first used during World War I in 1916) rumble across Europe,

crushing everything in their path. Ships called aircraft carriers are built with enormous flat decks so that aircraft can take off, land, and refuel, fighting anywhere over land and sea.

It is lucky for you that you are unable to see into the future. You would be horrified to know that not quite 83 years from the day you beat your drum at Fredericksburg, bombs called atomic bombs will be dropped on the cities of Hiroshima and Nagasaki in Japan. These bombs will kill more than 150,000 people. These 150,000 will be only part of the 50 million people who will die during World War II.

No war since 1945 has been fought on the same scale as World War II, but new technology has made weapons more powerful still. People are still inventing different ways to hurt their enemies. Battles and weapons in the future will likely be more deadly and cruel than those of today.

BROKEN CODES Keeping your battle plans secret from the enemy is vital. In World War II, plans and orders are sent by radio in code. This German code machine turns messages into code. After it is captured, Allies use it to help decode the German messages.

Prisoners of War

IT IS 1860, AND THE U.S. IS IN TURMOIL. States have been arguing for some time about whether slavery—owning other people and profiting from their labor—should or should not be legal.

Many Southern states are farming states, where cotton and tobacco are grown. Much of the farm work is done by slaves, originally brought from Africa. Most Northern states are more industrial, and slavery is illegal there.

Southerners worry that the U.S. government will make slavery illegal throughout the country. So eleven Southern states break off from the Union, as the United States is known, and form the Confederacy. To stop the country from breaking in two, the remaining Union states prepare to fight the Confederacy. The war begins in April 1861.

This painting shows three Confederate prisoners during the Civil War. They have been captured by Union soldiers during a battle at Petersburg, Virginia. Now they will spend the rest of the war in an unhealthy, crowded prison camp.

Inspecting the three weary prisoners is a Union officer. He is better dressed and armed than the Confederates. The Union has a far larger army. It also has more railroads to move and support its troops, and a large navy to stop foreign supplies from reaching Southern ports.

Despite these advantages, it will take the Union four terrible years to defeat the Confederacy. Some 620,000 men from both sides die. Much of the South is devastated, since most of the fighting takes place there. But America remains united, and, in the end, slavery is abolished.

PRISONERS FROM THE FRONT, 1866, WINSLOW HOMER

Winslow Homer (1836–1910)

Born in Boston, Winslow Homer is one of America's greatest artists. From 1861 to 1865, he drew pictures of the Civil War for the magazine *Harper's Weekly*. He used his battlefield drawings to paint *Prisoners from the Front* in oil after the end of the war. Later, Homer became well known for his beautiful pictures of the sea.

Beaten but proud This young man in his gray Confederate uniform has lost everything. He left his home and family to join the army and has been fighting for months, perhaps years. Now he is a prisoner. But with hand on hip and head thrown back, he faces the Union officer with pride and defiance.

Bare necessities This prisoner has a knapsack. If he is lucky, he will have some spare clothes and food in it. On top is his tin plate and cooking pot. Slung around his shoulder is a blanket which he will use to make his bed. Then and now soldiers often have to carry with them everything they need to live, as well as all their weapons.

Shiny shoes This Union officer has good reason to feel superior. His dark blue uniform is spotless, his leather boots gleam, and a fine sword hangs from his belt. Yet he regards his prisoners with pity. He knows what hardships they have suffered. He, too, wants this war to end.

Over the Top

IT IS A BITTERLY COLD DAY IN DECEMBER 1917. British soldiers have been ordered to attack the Germans. They must go "over the top" by climbing out of their trench and advancing across no-man's-land—the unoccupied area between their trench and the enemy's trench. Their uniforms show dark against the snow, so they are easy targets for the Germans. Many will be killed. The artist painted this scene later, but he was one of the men plodding grimly through the snow.

When this battle takes place, the war—later known as the First World War—has already lasted for over three years. At the start of the war in 1914, Germany invaded France and Belgium, countries allied with Britain. This created the western front, one of several major battlefronts where the war is fought. The United States joined the war on the French and British side in 1917.

Each army takes shelter from its opponents' devastating weapons by digging trenches. By 1915, the lines of trenches on the western front stretch continuously for 400 miles (650 km) from the English Channel to the Swiss border. The frontline trenches are supported by a network of other trenches stretching back from the front for several miles.

Soldiers on both sides live in the trenches in horrible conditions, often up to their knees in mud. Their clothes are infested with lice. The trenches are overrun with rats and littered with corpses.

Germany will surrender in November 1918. The war will have lasted four years. Over 65 million men will have fought in it; more than half will have been killed or wounded.

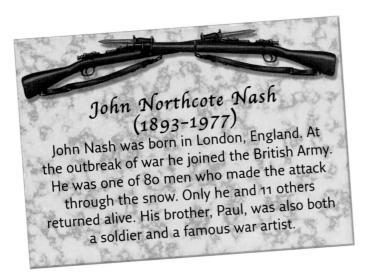

John Northcote Nash (1893–1977)

John Nash was born in London, England. At the outbreak of war he joined the British Army. He was one of 80 men who made the attack through the snow. Only he and 11 others returned alive. His brother, Paul, was also both a soldier and a famous war artist.

JOHN NASH

OVER THE TOP, 1918
JOHN NORTHCOTE NASH

Precarious pathway
Wooden boards like this are laid along the trench floor to keep the soldiers' feet dry and out of the mud. This is a temporary trench. Permanent ones are deeper, their walls often lined with wood. Periscopes (tube-shaped devices for seeing over obstructions) are also built into the wall so that lookouts can watch the enemy without being shot.

Unprepared attack This soldier, like his comrades, has had to climb up the muddy sides of the trench. This probably means that the attack has been launched in a hurry. In a well planned attack, soldiers use ladders to make sure they can climb out of their trenches quickly, no matter how much equipment they are carrying.

Vital protection This man's pack holds a gas mask to help him breathe in a poisonous gas attack. By 1917, every soldier in every army carries one. Poison gas burns the eyes and scorches lungs. Many victims choke to death. Soldiers injured by gas frequently suffer from its effects for the rest of their lives.

Heavy load These are ammunition pouches. British soldiers usually carry 100 or more bullets for their rifles. They often have to fight while carrying a lot of other equipment as well. In all, their load can weigh more than 60 pounds (27 kg).

Sharp and deadly A bayonet is a long knifelike blade that fits onto the end of a rifle. It is used when soldiers fight at close quarters in what is called hand-to-hand combat. Soldiers have to be trained to use bayonets because it is not easy to plunge a blade into another person, even in combat.

Wet feet Soldiers in the trenches often have to stand in muddy water for days on end, without even having a chance to change their socks. Many suffer from a crippling illness called "trench foot," which can rot feet and even require them to be amputated.

Beach Landing

IN 1944, AT THE HEIGHT OF WORLD WAR II, AMERICAN, BRITISH, AND OTHER ALLIED FORCES INVADE FRANCE IN A MILITARY OPERATION KNOWN AS D-DAY. France is occupied by Germany, under the leadership of the Nazi dictator Adolf Hitler. The Allies hope to end the German occupation.

German aggression plunged Europe into war in 1939. America joined the Allies in 1941. By 1944, the Allies are preparing a huge invasion force in Britain. Nearly 3,500,000 soldiers, including many Americans, are secretly gathering in camps along Britain's southern coast. Across the English Channel in France, German forces lie in wait for them behind massive defenses.

Early on the morning of June 6, 1944—a date that becomes known as D-Day—the vast invasion fleet reaches the coast of Normandy, France. Ahead of it, ships and aircraft bomb and shell the German defenses. Other Allied airplanes make sure the German Air Force cannot interfere. Airborne troops land first by parachute and glider to help capture the landing beaches.

As the fleet approaches the beaches, soldiers crouch in their landing craft. Many are seasick. All are frightened. On arrival, they wade ashore. Other landing craft bring tanks to join the fight. Thousands of men are killed and wounded by German gunfire. Those who survive—like the men in this painting—fight their way inland, where more tough battles will follow.

The Allied invasion will succeed, but it will take another year of fighting in Western Europe before Germany surrenders in May 1945.

BEACH LANDING (center panel from the D-Day triptych), 1945–1947, RICHARD ERNEST EURICH

Reaching the shore *These men are struggling through deep water, weighed down by their heavy equipment. Some men in the invasion force drown as soon as they get off their landing craft. Those that reach the beaches face death or injury from German guns and from explosives planted along the shoreline.*

Richard Ernest Eurich (1903–1992)

Richard Eurich was a British artist who painted many views of beaches and the sea. Some of these showed scenes from World War II. This painting is part of a triptych, a group of three images on the same subject. Triptych paintings more often show religious subjects.

Night attack *These are some of the 18,000 Allied parachutists who are dropped ahead of the main invasion force. In fact, they are dropped during the night before the landings from the sea, but the artist has shown the two events happening at the same time. Their job is to capture important road junctions, bridges, and gun batteries.*

Tin hat *Every soldier in World War II has a helmet similar to this one to wear in combat. Armies mostly stopped wearing armor of any kind in the 1600s, but helmets were reintroduced in World War I. They protect soldiers against artillery shells and other explosions, but they cannot keep bullets out.*

Glossary

archaeologist someone who studies how people lived in the past by examining things they left behind

archer a person who is skilled with a bow and arrow

armor protective clothes, usually made of metal, worn by soldiers in battle

atomic bomb a weapon that uses the huge energy held inside atoms to create a massive explosion

bayonet a dagger-like blade that can be attached to the end of a gun barrel and used in hand-to-hand combat

bolt a short, heavy arrow shot from a crossbow

bombardment an attack carried out by numerous guns or bombs on an enemy's position

cannon a large gun that fires iron or stone balls

castle a large, strong building or group of buildings surrounded by a high wall for protection

catapult a large sling-like weapon used to hurl missiles at the enemy

cavalry soldiers who fight on horseback

chain mail small iron rings linked to form a protective layer of clothing for a soldier

crossbow a very powerful type of bow mounted on a wooden frame

Crusades a series of wars in which Christian armies tried to capture the Holy Land from its Muslim rulers

empire a group of countries ruled by one person, called an emperor

gunpowder an explosive substance used to fire guns and make bombs. Gunpowder is a mixture of potassium nitrate, charcoal, and sulfur

illuminated manuscript a book with pictures, written and painted by hand

infantry soldiers who fight on foot

Timeline

1073–1083 Bayeux Tapestry created (pp.20–23)

c. 1332–1322 B.C. Wooden chest painted (pp.6–7)

2nd century B.C. Mosaic of the Battle of Issus created (pp.10–13)

1096–99 First Crusade

1200s Illustrated songbook showing battle between Muslims and Christians created (pp.24–27)

1400 B.C.

200 B.C.

200 A.D.

1000

1200

1400

1600

356 B.C. Alexander the Great born

c. 800s Stirrups first used in Europe

1200s English longbow in general use

late 1300s First cannons used in Europe

late 1500s Flintlock musket invented

246 B.C. Emperor Shi Huangdi orders work to begin on his tomb (pp.8–9)

c. 250 A.D. Ludovisi Battle Sarcophagus created (pp.14–17)

early 1300s Gunpowder arrives in Europe from China

1400s *The Battle of Crécy* is painted (pp.28–31)

javelin a spear that can be thrown or used for stabbing

knight a fighting man who serves his lord or king when called upon to do so, usually wearing armor and fighting on horseback

lance a long pointed wooden weapon used by knights and other cavalrymen

legionary a soldier in a legion

legion one of the main military units in the Ancient Roman army

longbow a type of plain wooden bow used by English soldiers in the Middle Ages

lord a wealthy landowner who is often a knight as well

mace a club-like weapon

machine gun an automatic weapon used to fire bullets rapidly and continuously

mosaic a picture or design made up of small pieces of glass or stone adhered to a surface

musket a gun similar to a modern rifle, but less accurate and more difficult to load

nobleman someone born into the highest social class (the nobility)

phalanx a close formation of infantry spearmen used by Alexander the Great's army

pharaoh a king of Ancient Egypt

professional army an army made up of soldiers trained and paid by the government of a country

sling a weapon made of a strip of cloth or leather and used to throw stones

submachine gun a type of machine gun light enough to be carried by a soldier

tactics the system or way of organizing troops in combat

tank an armored vehicle moving on caterpillar tracks and armed with guns

telegraph a system used for sending messages by wire

1786 John Trumbull paints *The Battle of Bunker (or Bunker's) Hill* (pp.34–37)

1721 Rifles introduced to North America

1862 Gatling gun invented

1855 François-Auguste Biard paints *On the Deck During a Sea Battle* (pp.42–45)

1876 Battle of Little Big Horn. Twenty years later, c.1900, Amos Bad Heart Bull paints *Retreat of Major Marcus Reno's Command* (pp.54–57)

1918 John Northcote Nash paints *Over the Top* (pp.54–57)

1700 — 1775–1783 American Revolution — 1800 — 1900 — 1950

1835 Colt revolver developed

1861–1865 American Civil War

1914–1918 World War I

1939–1945 World War II

1917–1920 Thompson submachine gun developed

1789 Claude Cholat paints *The Storming of the Bastille* (pp.38–41)

1866 Winslow Homer paints *Prisoners from the Front* (pp.52–53)

1945-1947 Richard Ernest Eurich paints *Beach Landing* (pp.58–59)

Further reading

Adams, Simon. *World War One.* Eyewitness series. New York: Dorling Kindersley, 2004.

Biesty, Stephen and Richard Platt. *Man-of-War.* Stephen Biesty's Cross-Sections series. New York: Dorling Kindersley, 1993.

Byam, Michèle. *Arms and Armor.* Eyewitness series. New York: Dorling Kindersley, 2004.

Cotterell, Arthur. *Ancient China.* Eyewitness series. New York: Dorling Kindersley, 2005.

DK Publishing. *Ancient Greece.* New York: Dorling Kindersley, 2004.

DK Publishing. *Knight.* New York: Dorling Kindersley, 2004.

Gay, Kathlyn. *Silent Death: The Threat of Biological and Chemical Warfare.* Exceptional Social Studies Titles for Upper Grades series. Brookfield, CT: Twenty-First Century Books, 2001.

Grant, R. G.. *Battle: A Visual Journey Through 5,000 Years of Combat.* New York: Dorling Kindersley, 2005.

Hatt, Christine. *The American West: Native Americans, Pioneers and Settlers.* History in Writing series. London: Evans Brothers Ltd., 1998.

Hatt, Christine. *The First World War, 1914–1918.* History in Writing series. London: Evans Brothers Ltd., 2000.

Macdonald, Fiona. *Ancient Egyptians.* Hauppauge, NY: Barron's, 1993.

Morris, Neil. *Everyday Life in Ancient Egypt.* Mankato, MN: Smart Apple Media, 2004.

Platt, Richard. *D-Day Landings: The Story of the Allied Invasion.* DK Readers series. New York: Dorling Kindersley, 2004.

Woods, Michael and Mary B. Woods. *Ancient Warfare: From Clubs to Catapults.* Ancient Technology series. Minneapolis: Runestone Press, 2000.

Websites

History of War and Warfare
http://www.bbc.co.uk/history/forkids
The British Broadcasting Corporation's website offers resources on world history, ancient and modern, including sections devoted to World War I and the lives of children during World War II.

http://www.pbs.org/civilwar/images/
This section of the PBS website for Ken Burns's documentary "The Civil War" highlights details of photographs and other images from the American Civil War.

http://www.warmuseum.ca
The website of the Canadian War Museum, Ottawa, Ontario, includes the online adventure game "Over the Top," which depicts the bravery and horrors of World War I, as experienced by Canadian soldiers fighting in the trenches of Europe.

Arms and Armor
http://www.clevelandart.org/kids/armor/
The website of the Cleveland Museum of Art displays photographs from the museum's collection of armor, crossbows, maces, and swords.

More about the Art in this Book
www.bayeuxtapestry.org.uk
This site explains in detail what is happening in each section of the Bayeux Tapestry.

Index

Picture credits

1 Detail from Battle between Crusaders and Muslims on page 25. **2,3** Detail from *Bayeux Tapestry* on pages 20-21. **3** Detail of funerary model of marching soldiers from tomb of Mesehti, Assyut on pages 4-5, TR; Detail of armor on page, 19, ML; *Mons Meg* cannon on page 32, MR; The Gatling gun on page 50, BL. **4** Funerary model of marching soldiers from the Tomb of Mesehti, Assyut, Egyptian National Museum, Cairo/Bridgeman Art Library, background and B. **5**. Corinthian helmet (bronze)/Private Collection/Bridgeman Art Library, T; Roman legionary's sword/British Museum, B. **6-7** Detail from lid of box of stuccoed wood, from the tomb of Tutankhamen/Robert Harding. **8-9** *The Terra-cotta Army*, from the tomb of the First Emperor of China, Qin Shi Huang, Xian, Shaanxi Province, China/Robert Harding/Gavin Hellier. **10-11** *The Alexander Mosaic*, depicting the Battle of Issus/Museo Archeologico Nazionale, Naples, Italy/Bridgeman Art Library. **12-13** Details from *The Alexander Mosaic* on pages 10-11. **14-15** *The Ludovisi Sarcophagus*/ Terme Museum, Rome/Bridgeman Art Library. **16-17** Details from *The Ludovisi Sarcophagus* on pages 14-15. **18-19** South German hunting crossbow, early 16th century/Indian elephant armor, *circa* early 17th

century/North German suit of armor, *circa* 1535 and small suit of armor for child, *circa* 1630 Courtesy of the Board of Trustees of the Armouries. **20-21** The Bayeux Tapestry/Musée de la Tapisserie, Bayeux/Bridgeman Art Library. **22-23** Details from The Bayeux Tapestry on pages 20-21. **24** Battle between Crusaders and Muslims, illumination, folio 92R from *Canticles of Saint Mary*, 13th century manuscript for Alfonso X 'The Wise'/Biblioteca Monasterio del Escorial/Dagli Orti/The Art Archive. **25** Battle between Crusaders and Muslims, illumination, folio 92R from *Canticles of Saint Mary*, 13th century manuscript for Alfonso X 'The Wise'/Biblioteca Monasterio del Escorial/Bildarchiv Steffens/Bridgeman Art Library. **26** Details from Battle between Crusaders and Muslims on page 24, The Art Archive, BL, MR; Bridgeman Art Library, BM. **27** Details from Battle between Crusaders and Muslims on page 25, The Art Archive, BL; Bridgeman Art Library, MR. **28-29** *The Battle of Crécy, 1346*, from Froissart's *Chronicles*, Fr 2643 f.165v, French School, 15th century/Bibliothèque Nationale, Paris/Bridgeman Art Library. **30-31** Details from *The Battle of Crécy* on pages, 28-29. **32-33** *Mons Meg*, cannon, *circa* 1450/Crown Copyright 2006/Historic Scotland Images, background and ML; German hunting flintlock musket, 1646/Courtesy of the Board of Trustees of the Armouries, B. **33** Colt revolver/Private Collection/

Bridgeman Art Library, TR. **34-35** *The Death of General Warren at the Battle of Bunker's Hill, 17 June, 1775*, oil on canvas, by John Trumbull (American, 1756–1843). Museum of Fine Arts, Boston. Gift of Howland S. Warren 1977.853. © 2006 Museum of Fine Arts, Boston. All rights reserved/Bridgeman Art Library. **36-37** Details from *The Death of General Warren at the Battle of Bunker's Hill* on pages 34-35. **38-39** *The Siege of the Bastille, 1789*, gouache on card by Claude Cholat/Musée de la Ville de Paris, Musée Carnavalet, Paris/Lauros/Giraudon/Bridgeman Art Library. **40-41** Details from *The Siege of the Bastille, 1789* on pages 38-39. **42-43** *On the Deck during a Sea Battle*, 1855, oil on canvas by François-Auguste Biard/Central Naval Museum, St. Petersburg, Russia/Bridgeman Art Library. **44-45** Details from *On the Deck during a Sea battle* on pages 42-43. **46-47** *Retreat of Major Marcus Reno's Command*, ink on paper, by Amos Bad Heart Bull/Private Collection/The Stapleton Collection/Bridgeman Art Library. **48-49** Details from *Retreat of Major Marcus Reno's Command* on pages 46-47. **50-51** The Gatling gun/Courtesy of the Board of Trustees of the Armouries. **51** Thompson submachine gun/ Courtesy of the Board of Trustees of the Armouries, T; Enigma Machine/ Bletchley Park: www.bletchleypark.org.uk, B. **52** *Prisoners from the Front*, oil on canvas,1866, by Winslow Homer: The Metropolitan Museum of Art,

Gift of Mrs. Frank B. Porter, 1922 (22.207) Photograph © 1995 The Metropolitan Museum of Art. **53** Details from *Prisoners from the Front* on page 52. **54-55** *Over the Top, 1st Artists' Rifles at Marcoing, 30th December 1917*, by John Northcote Nash/© Imperial War Museum, London/Bridgeman Art Library. **56-57** Details from, *Over The Top* on pages 54-55. **58** *Beach Landing*, center panel from the D-Day triptych, 1944, oil on panel, by Richard Ernest Eurich/© Harris Museum and Art Gallery, Preston, Lancashire/Bridgeman Art Library. **59** Details from *Beach Landing* on page 58.

Front cover: Detail from *The Death of General Warren at the Battle of Bunker's Hill, 17 June, 1775*, oil on canvas, by John Trumbull (American, 1756-1843). Museum of Fine Arts, Boston. Gift of Howland S. Warren 1977.853. © 2006 Museum of Fine Arts, Boston. All rights reserved. **Back cover:** Detail from *On the Deck during a Sea Battle*, 1855, oil on canvas by François-Auguste Biard/Central Naval Museum, St. Petersburg, Russia/Bridgeman Art Library, BL; Detail from the Bayeux Tapestry/Musée de la Tapisserie, Bayeux/Bridgeman Art Library, BR. **Front and Back cover:** Background, fragment of chain mail shirt, late 15th or early 16th century/Courtesy of the Board of Trustees of the Armouries.